CONTENTS

A BOY AND HIS BEAR
By Harriet Graham

ABOUT THE SERIES
INSIDE FRONT COVER

BACKGROUND INFORMATION
3–5

LESSON PLANS
6–19

INVESTIGATING THE COVER	6
WHO IS DICKON?	6
FOLLOWING DICKON THROUGH THE STREETS OF ELIZABETHAN LONDON	8
THE BEAR CUB	9
THE VOICE OF THE BEAR CUB	10
JACOB, HIS OPINIONS AND HIS SPEECH	11
ELIZABETHAN LONDON – THE TIME AND PLACE	12
SUPERSTITION	13
SHAKESPEARE'S WORLD	14
THE ESCAPE TO FRANCE	15
CAPTURE AND FREEDOM	17
THE END AND THE FUTURE	18
'MY MOTHER SAW A DANCING BEAR' BY CHARLES CAUSLEY	19

PHOTOCOPIABLES
20–32

PROLOGUE: IN THE BEGINNING...	20
EXPLORING DICKON'S CHARACTER	21
EXPLORING DICKON'S CHARACTER: EXTENSION	22
GLOSSARY	23
MEMORIES AND THE PAST (1)	24
MEMORIES AND THE PAST (2)	25
DICKON'S THOUGHTS ABOUT THE BEAR CUB	26
READING THE BEAR CUB'S THOUGHTS	27
SHOULD DICKON BE INVOLVED WITH THE BEAR CUB?	28
HOW DO WE KNOW THE STORY IS SET IN ELIZABETHAN ENGLAND?	29
LOOKING CLOSELY AT DESCRIPTION	30
WHAT DO SEBASTIEN, ROSA AND BRUNO THINK OF DICKON?	31
WRITING A BLURB FOR THE BOOK COVER	32

SKILLS GRID
INSIDE BACK COVER

CREDITS

Published by Scholastic Ltd,
Villiers House,
Clarendon Avenue,
Leamington Spa,
Warwickshire CV32 5PR
Text © Fiona Collins
© 1998 Scholastic Ltd
1 2 3 4 5 6 7 8 9 0   8 9 0 1 2 3 4 5 6 7

Author Fiona Collins
Series consultant Fiona Collins
Editor Jane Bishop
Series designer Lynne Joesbury
Designer Lynne Joesbury
Illustrations Jane Bottomley
Cover illustration Helen Cooper

Designed using Adobe Pagemaker

British Library Cataloguing-in-Publication Data
A catalogue record for this book is available from the British Library.

ISBN 0-590-54707-0

The right of Fiona Collins to be identified as the Author of this work has been asserted by her in accordance with the Copyright, Designs and Patents Act 1988.

All rights reserved. This book is sold subject to the condition that it shall not, by way of trade or otherwise, be lent, hired out or otherwise circulated without the publisher's prior consent in any form of binding or cover other than that in which it is published and without a similar condition, including this condition, being imposed upon the subsequent purchaser.

No part of this publication may be reproduced, stored in a retrieval system, or transmitted, in any form or by any means, electronic, mechanical, photocopying, recording or otherwise, without the prior permission of the publisher. This book remains copyright, although permission is granted to copy pages 20 to 32 for classroom distribution and use only in the school which has purchased the book and in accordance with the CLA licensing agreement. Photocopying permission is given for purchasers only and not for borrowers of books from any lending service.

ACKNOWLEDGEMENTS

David Higham Associates for the use of 'My Mother Saw a Dancing Bear' from *Figgie Hobbin* by Charles Causley © 1970, Charles Causley (1970, Macmillan)
Museum of London for the use of Braun and Hogenberg's map of London Ref CL98/2624 © Museum of London
Penguin Limited for the use of text from 'The Winter's Tale' by Leon Garfield from *Shakespeare Stories II* by Leon Garfield © 1994, Leon Garfield (1994, Victor Gollancz/Hamish Hamilton)
Every effort has been made to trace copyright holders and the publishers apologize for any inadvertent omissions.

BACKGROUND INFORMATION

GENRE

A Boy and His Bear is historical fiction, which means that the story is set in a definite period in history and that the characters are involved in a conflict or dilemma that is realistic for that period. It provides valuable background details about the time in which it is set – the places, events and characters – and, as a result, may extend the knowledge readers already have of the period. *A Boy and His Bear* begins in London at the beginning of the seventeenth century and concludes in South-West France. Like all good historical fiction, *A Boy and His Bear* has been well researched and is historically accurate. It also has a gripping, well-paced plot and realistically developed characters.

PLOT SUMMARY

The narrative centres on a young boy, Dickon, who has been unwillingly apprenticed, by his stepfather, to a tannery in Southwark. He is a bright, literate boy and one day he is asked to take a letter to the Master of the Bear Garden on Bankside. On the way he meets the Bear Catcher and then inadvertently befriends a bear cub. He calms the cub by showing it kindness and gentleness which is mistaken for magic and sorcery by some jealous onlookers.

The story then focuses on Dickon's desire to save the cub from the bear-baiting ring and facing a cruel and painful death. At one point in the narrative, Dickon actually watches bear baiting himself, which he finds extremely upsetting. Dickon saves the cub from the Bear Master and, with the help of Jacob an old servant of his father's, manages to escape to France with a troupe of acrobats. They spend the winter in the mountains in South-West France, practising their tumbling routines and hoping that Dickon will be able to teach the bear cub to dance to give their act an added attraction.

The story reaches its climax when the Bear Catcher finds them and kidnaps Dickon, the bear cub and Rosa, a young acrobat. At the end of the story, the bear cub helps to save Dickon and Rosa from the Bear Catcher and thereby earns his freedom. Dickon is invited to stay with the acrobat troupe and play the flute for them at their performances.

ABOUT THE AUTHOR

Harriet Graham, has published twelve books for children, although unfortunately only *A Boy and His Bear* is still in print. She is a grandmother and lives in West London beside the River Thames.

Harriet Graham says that she enjoys researching for her writing and finds it interesting and stimulating. She has a particular interest in Shakespeare's London and her research for *A Boy and His Bear* took her to the Bear Garden Museum on Bankside.

In her role as a children's writer, she visits schools to talk and read to pupils. She says of *A Boy and His Bear*: '... it reads aloud rather well and does seem to hold their (the pupil's) attention, and I have had some really interesting and wide-ranging questions afterwards.'

SPECIFIC TEACHING OPPORTUNITIES
TEXT LEVEL
ISSUES AND THEMES

The book raises many issues and themes. By setting most of the story in Elizabethan London, Harriet Graham allows the cruelty of bear baiting to be

BACKGROUND INFORMATION

viewed in context. However, it is an important issue to discuss with the children. The time and place are described effectively, through descriptions of London alleys, buildings and the river.

The inclusion of Southwark Fair and the description of its many food stalls also helps to give the reader a flavour of the time. In addition, the author makes reference to the Globe Theatre and the inclusion of the character of 'Will' in Chapter 9 adds to the realistic nature of the narrative.

CHARACTERS

All the characters in the story are believable, although the evil characters, such as Osric and the Bear Catcher, are stereotypical. The good characters are sympathetic and support Dickon well. Dickon's friendship with Rosa, towards the end of the story, means that he is not left alone when the bear cub leaves. The author has included at least one character who is not so easily defined, that of Bruno. Dickon does not like him initially, he mistrusts him, but Bruno turns out to be supportive of Dickon in the end. This twist allows children to understand that not all characters in books have to be so clear cut, and can be more like the people in real life.

NARRATIVE

An interesting aspect of the story is that it is told through two narrators. The main narrator tells Dickon's story in the third person. It is through this voice that we learn about Dickon's past, his thoughts and feelings and what happens to him. The second, and less-used narrative voice tells the story of the bear cub, as a first-person narrative. The author has used italics to identify the bear's narration and to show the difference between the two.

The language of the bear cub's narration is more simplistic than the third-person narrative, and helps to give the reader an insight into the mind of the bear. It is worth noting how the tone of the bear's narration changes as the cub grows up. It changes from at first being dependent on its mother to trusting Dickon, realizing that Dickon is kind and trying to help him.

By using the technique of two narrators, the author gives the reader the opportunity to understand the story from both perspectives and provides two different points of view.

SENTENCE LEVEL

As Dickon is confronted by the problem of saving the bear cub from the cruelty of the Bear Garden, the reader sees Dickon's shifting thoughts and dilemmas through the use of carefully placed punctuation and a mixture of simple and complex sentences. The dialogue, which reflects the speech patterns of the historical period, offers opportunities to look at the organic nature of the English language – how it changes over time. Some of the dialogue in the book also highlights the use of non-standard English.

WORD LEVEL

Language and vocabulary from the Elizabethan period is used to set the scene for the reader. People are often addressed with titles that reflect their social position, such as Master or Mistress. A variety of different words are used with which children would be unfamiliar with today, for example *whelp, curfew, surcoat, sorcery*. All of this supports study of word origins and the development of language. Within descriptions, there is use of figurative language such as simile, metaphor, alliteration and extended noun phrases, which also add to the reader's understanding of the time and place in which the story is set.

BACKGROUND INFORMATION

THE ACTIVITIES

The activities aim to involve the children in work which encourages them to explore the novel at text, sentence and word level, thereby covering many of the requirements for years 5 and 6 of the National Literacy Strategy *Framework for Teaching*. Activities have also been designed to encourage the children to write in different styles and for different purposes, for example to engage in argument, to write poetry and to write using another narrative voice.

THE POSTER

The poster should be used as a whole-class teaching resource to support the activities in this book.

SIDE 1

This depicts part of a 1580 map of London to show the children the size and layout of the city of London in the seventeenth century, and also to illustrate the places Dickon visited. The map does not show the Globe Theatre as this was not built until 1598, when it was situated to the right of the Bear Garden. Scenes from *A Boy and His Bear* are also shown on this side.

SIDE 2

The two extracts on the poster from Shakespeare's *A Winter's Tale* are included to support the understanding that bear dancing and bear baiting were very popular in Elizabethan times. Apparently, Shakespeare included the bear at the end of Act Three of his play because he wanted to give a famous bear, from the Bear Garden, a walk-on part!

The Charles Causley poem, 'My Mother saw a Dancing Bear', provides a contrast with the end of the story. The bear in the Causley poem can only dream of freedom while Nounou, the bear cub in *A Boy and His Bear*, earns his freedom at the end of the story. The poem is included to complete the unit of work on *A Boy and His Bear* and engage the children in the poetic form.

LINKED RESOURCES
SAME PERIOD

The Terrible Tudors by Terry Deary Horrible Histories series (Scholastic Hippo)
Children of Winter by Berlie Doherty (Mammoth)
Astercote by Penelope Lively (Mammoth)
My Friend Walter by Michael Morpurgo (Mammoth)
The Armourer's House by Rosemary Sutcliffe (Red Fox)
A Traveller in Time by Alison Uttley (Puffin)

SAME THEME

Keeping Henry by Nina Bawden (Puffin)
The Midnight Fox by Betsy Byars (Puffin)
The Great Elephant Chase by Gillian Cross (Puffin)
The Dancing Bear Michael Morpurgo (Young Lions)
Blitzcat by Robert Westall (Pan)

ADDRESSES

The Museum of London, London Wall, London EC2Y 5HN
Shakespeare's Globe Theatre, 21 New Globe Walk, London SE1 9DT

LESSON PLANS

BEFORE READING

INVESTIGATING THE COVER
RESOURCES NEEDED

Poster, back cover of the book copied onto an overhead transparency (OHT) (optional), flip chart, photocopiable page 20, writing materials, dictionaries.

WHOLE-CLASS WORK

Introduce *A Boy and His Bear* to the class by using the poster to set the scene in relation to seventeenth-century London. Talk to the children about Queen Elizabeth I and what life was like for most people during her reign. The children may have studied the Tudors earlier in primary school and this is a good opportunity to remind them about the period.

From this discussion, which sets up the historical context, move on to talk about some specific points relating to the front cover of the book. Ask the children to brainstorm the feelings they have about the bear: discuss the rope that is tied around its neck and the look on its face. Link this with the words at the bottom of the front cover: 'I shan't let him fight. Not ever ...' Ask the children to consider who might be saying this – Who is 'I'? Use the opportunity to discuss the Tudors' attitude to wild animals and in particular the widespread abuse of wild bears, including bear baiting and bear dancing.

Now look at the blurb on the back cover. It may be useful to copy this onto an OHT so that all the children can read it. Ensure that the children understand the term 'blurb'. Discuss with the class what can be learned from the blurb and what questions it provokes from the reader, for example: What is a tanner's apprentice? What are the terrible dangers they face? Record these questions on a chart and refer to them during the reading.

GROUP WORK

Children can work in mixed-ability or differentiated groups, as differentiation is by outcome in this guided reading task. Building on the class discussion, ask the children to read the 'Prologue' together and to summarize the main points, using photocopiable page 20, 'Prologue: in the beginning...', as a framework.

PLENARY

Ask different groups to share their summaries of the 'Prologue'. As they report back with their answers, record the children's predictions, ask them why they have predicted a particular outcome and discuss the range. Display the predictions so that they can be referred to during the course of reading.

DURING READING

WHO IS DICKON?
PLOT SUMMARY: CHAPTER ONE

Chapter One is very important as the narrator introduces Dickon, the main character, gives details about his family background and also introduces the reader to other significant characters, such as Master Nashe, Ned and Ann. The story is set around 1600 in London. We learn that Dickon's father has died and as a result, Dickon's education has been stopped. The boy has been apprenticed to a tannery by his stepfather. Dickon's life at the tannery is miserable. He is bullied and picked on constantly. The chapter ends with him being summoned by the Master – for a beating, Dickon assumes.

RESOURCES NEEDED

Photocopiable page 23, dictionaries, poster, photocopiable pages 21 and 22 as individual activity sheets for guided group work.

LESSON PLANS

WHOLE-CLASS WORK

Read the first chapter to the whole class and, as you read, discuss particular words and phrases to encourage further understanding, such as: *tannery, gabled house, merchant, apprenticed, milksop, litany, curfew, carcasses*. It is important to discuss these words in context so that the children understand their actual meaning within the text. Photocopiable page 23 'Glossary', provides a glossary for the children to complete as they find the different words in the story.

In this first chapter, places in London are also mentioned, such as Eastcheap, Southwark and London Bridge. The map on the poster will help you identify where these are for the children.

After reading the chapter, discuss the plot so far with the class. Who is Dickon? Why is he an apprentice in a tannery? What happened to his father? Who is Master Tyndal? You might also ask the children to identify any clues to show that the story is not set in the present time.

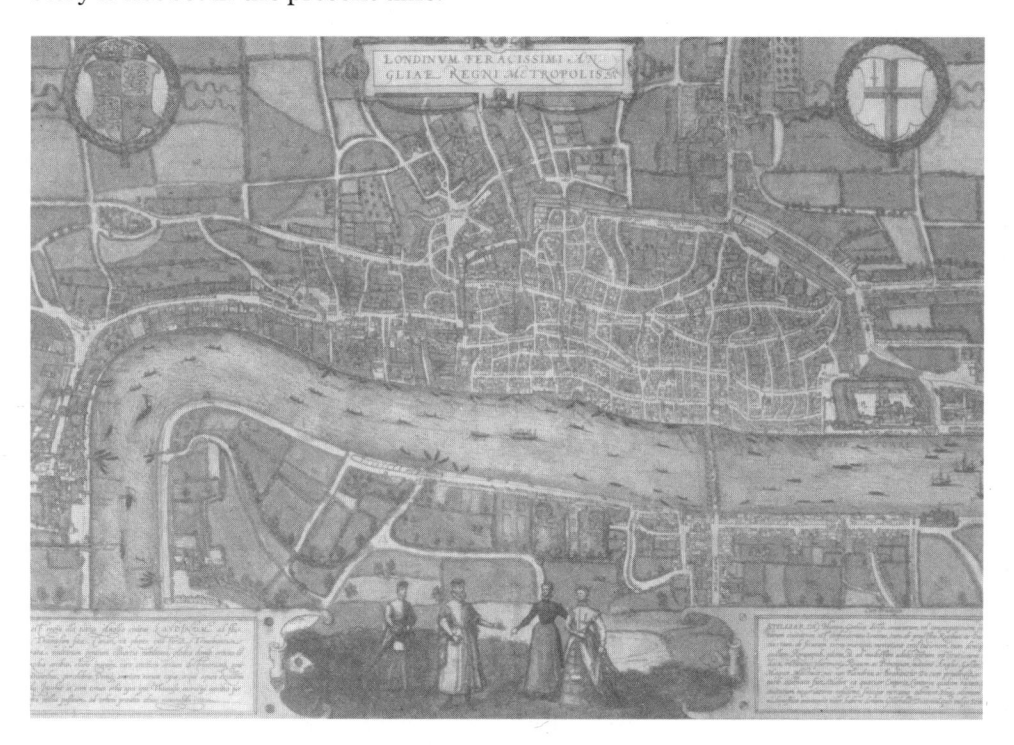

GROUP WORK

Ask the groups to consider how the author has described the main character and his different relationships. Give each group at least one copy of the novel to refer to, and each pupil should also have a copy of photocopiable page 21, 'Exploring Dickon's character', for individual work. Encourage them to discuss the sheet with their peers.

All the groups should work through the photocopiable sheet and more able children can also complete the extension activity on page 22, 'Exploring Dickon's character: extension'. The last question on the extension photocopiable sheet asks children to find out in what other children's novel a character called Dickon appears. The answer is, in *The Secret Garden* by Frances Hodgson Burnett, written in 1911.

PLENARY

Following the group work, conduct a class discussion about different aspects of Dickon's character and descriptions that the author uses to build up our picture of him. You might focus on the aspect of laziness and discuss what this means, and whether the different groups feel that this is a fair comment about Dickon.

LESSON PLANS

FOLLOWING DICKON THROUGH THE STREETS OF ELIZABETHAN LONDON

PLOT SUMMARY: CHAPTER TWO

Dickon is not whipped by Master Nashe but instead he is asked to write down a letter for him and deliver it to the Master of the Bear Pit, just past London Bridge. We go with Dickon through the back streets to the Bear Garden and on the way meet the sinister Bear Catcher who is going there with his wagon carrying a she-bear and her young cub.

RESOURCES NEEDED

Poster, photocopiable pages 24 and 25, prepared as OHTs if possible, flip chart.

WHOLE-CLASS WORK

As you read Chapter Two with the children, ask them how they think Dickon felt when he realized he was not going to be whipped, but instead was asked to scribe a letter and deliver it to the Master of the Bear Pit.

From the tannery, the reader accompanies Dickon through the streets of London. Encourage the children to refer to the map on the poster as a visual aid. During this journey some of Dickon's past is revealed.

Harriet Graham achieves this by using an object from the present to evoke the past. The setting for Dickon's meeting with his sister Ann is a churchyard. Here they see their father's overgrown gravestone which triggers memories about their father for both of them.

Discuss with the class the two extracts that you have prepared on OHTs – photocopiable page 24 'Memories and the Past (1)' and page 25 'Memories and the Past (2)'. Talk to them about the methods that Harriet Graham has used to give readers information about events from the characters' pasts.

In the first extract, the author uses:

* the setting of the churchyard as a link that Dickon and his sister have with the past: their father is buried in this churchyard. From this we learn how Dickon regularly meets his sister there and what they do when they meet
* the dialogue that takes place between Dickon and Ann about their father's gravestone to provide the reader with additional information. From this we learn when their father died, that he was a merchant and also a little of what their family life was like.

In the second extract, the author:

* uses dialogue to tell us what the old family servant, Jacob, is doing now
* links a memory with the conversation between brother and sister, revealing the sort of relationship they had with Jacob in the past.

Thus in both extracts the present is used to provide an insight into the past.

To conclude this session, focus again on the second extract and discuss the way punctuation is used in setting out dialogue. As you discuss this with the children, record the information that is discovered on the flip chart and keep this on display for further use later.

GROUP WORK

Ask the children to re-read the last paragraph of Chapter Two, and to think about Dickon, writing a recount of what his thoughts

LESSON PLANS

were at the end of the chapter, when he heard '... a deep throated, terrible roar'. They should write it as if they were Dickon, in the first person. Advise them to consider what his thoughts and his feelings were in the situation. Ask the children to write for fifteen or twenty minutes and then re-read and check their work for five minutes, ready to share it with the rest of the class. Differentiation for this activity will occur through outcome.

PLENARY

Rather than asking individuals to read complete passages, ask the children to share phrases, sentences and short extracts from their pieces. Individual words might also be discussed. Finish with the question – What now?

THE BEAR CUB
PLOT SUMMARY: CHAPTER THREE

Dickon meets the Bear Catcher outside the Bear Garden, when the Catcher asks him to hold the reins of his wagon. Dickon then goes on to the Bear Garden to give the letter to the Master. The bear wagon enters the Garden and Dickon sees an enormous she-bear taken out. As he watches, a bear cub suddenly appears and runs towards Dickon, who calms it down. Dickon's control over the bear cub surprises and impresses the Bear Master – so much so that, by the end of his visit, Dickon has been persuaded to visit the cub every Sunday, on his day off, to tame it and teach it to dance and perform tricks in order to stop it from being killed by the Bear Master's dogs.

BACKGROUND INFORMATION

Today we believe bear baiting to be inhumane, but the Elizabethans thought it was a wonderful sport. Wild bears were imported into Britain for baiting, which was held regularly in London. The bear was tied to a stake by a long rope and fierce dogs, such as mastiffs, were let into the ring to attack it.

RESOURCES NEEDED

Photocopiable page 26, writing materials.

WHOLE-CLASS WORK

As you read Chapter Three, ask the children to build up a picture of the different characters that Dickon meets. Discuss each character in turn and ask the children what information they base their opinions on.
For example:
* The Bear Catcher is described with a whip in his hand and flecks of blood on his hands.
* The Master of the Bear Garden is described as 'a portly figure wearing a fur-trimmed surcoat hurrying towards them.' He is anxious about the Bear Catcher and is abrupt and to the point in his tone.
* Osric, of whom we are given a short glimpse, does not give Dickon a clear answer when he first meets him, and talks to him 'through narrowed eyes' and makes fun of Dickon in front of the Master – 'Most important, so he says,' drawled Osric.

Encourage the children to use the inferences in the text to make deductions as to what sort of characters they are and what part they will play, if any, in the rest of the story. Draw their attention to the way in which each character speaks, for example: *drawled, laughed, said slyly*.

Finish the class work by discussing what Dickon did to calm the bear cub. Was it magic or just kindness?

LESSON PLANS

GROUP WORK

The narrator plays an important role at the end of this chapter, as the reader is shown how Dickon decides what to do about the bear cub. Discuss the passage with the children in their differentiated groups and then tell them to work on photocopiable page 26, 'Dickon's thoughts about the bear cub'. For the more able pupils, once they have completed the activity sheet, ask them to investigate the author's use of punctuation and complex sentences and how these reflect Dickon's thoughts. Less able pupils may need teacher support to read and discuss the piece first, and perhaps they can then independently to highlight the significant aspects on the sheet itself.

A further extension activity could be to ask the children to write a short passage to reflect Dickon's thoughts on his way back to the tannery.

PLENARY

Through this initial work on narrative voice, discuss the role of the narrator and show how the main narrator is focusing on Dickon.

THE VOICE OF THE BEAR CUB
PLOT SUMMARY: CHAPTER FOUR

At the beginning of Chapter Four we are given the cub's perspective on the situation at the Bear Garden. The scene then moves to the tannery, where Dickon, thinking constantly about the bear cub, is being badly treated as usual. On the following Sunday, he meets Ann in the churchyard and tells her about the cub. She is not in favour of his helping it. But Dickon goes to the Bear Garden just the same and the cub shows he is pleased to see Dickon. But while they are playing, Dickon is being watched secretly.

RESOURCES NEEDED

Photocopiable page 27, writing materials.

WHOLE-CLASS WORK

Start this session by discussing what is going on in Dickon's life at the time. He dislikes the tannery, Ann is worried about him and he constantly thinks about the cub. Twice in this chapter the reader is introduced to the voice of the bear cub. Read the beginning of the chapter aloud to the class and discuss how the bear's narration differs from that of the third-person narrator. The most obvious aspect is that it is in the first person, but the language also differs, for example 'The brightness has gone from the skies now' and 'In the black time the beasts with two legs are asleep'. Go through this initial passage, identify particular phrases and discuss with the children how another narrator might write them. The bear narrator relates his feelings to his previous world and environment. He tells of the day passing, the pain, language and sleeping. The language used is simile, until he describes the mountains and here it becomes more poetic and imaginative to represent his feelings. From this analysis, discuss why Harriet Graham has used such language and style and what effect this has on the reader. Then read to the end of the chapter, if there is time.

GROUP WORK

At the end of Chapter Four, Dickon has come back to the bear cub, but the reader only sees the situation from the cub's perspective. Working in differentiated groups, with photocopiable page 27, 'Reading the bear cub's thoughts', ask the children to focus on the bear's narration at the end of the chapter. Two aspects are looked at

LESSON PLANS

in depth: first identifying what Dickon did to the cub to win the cub's trust and secondly identifying the use of figurative language in the piece. More able children might be asked to consider why this other narrative has been included in the story and to write down their ideas.

PLENARY

As a whole class, focus on similes and ask the children why they think authors use them. Share some of the examples from the group work, evaluating how well they have used the link with the countryside. Finish with discussing what the children think about the use of two narrators.

JACOB, HIS OPINIONS AND HIS SPEECH
PLOT SUMMARY: CHAPTER FIVE

On the way home from the Bear Garden, Dickon meets Jacob, who was once his father's servant. Jacob knows about the cub from Ann and he tries to persuade Dickon not to become involved. Back at the tannery, Ned talks about nothing but the forthcoming Southwark Fair. The week goes slowly and Dickon is very excited at the thought of seeing the cub again. But on Friday, Dickon is told that on Monday he will start working with the knife in the tannery, something he dreads.

RESOURCES NEEDED

Flip chart displaying some of the phrases Jacob uses (see below), photocopiable page 28, writing materials.

WHOLE-CLASS WORK

Following the reading of Chapter Five, look in detail with the class at the way Jacob speaks in pages 65–70. Focus on the following:
* Vocabulary: *grown a fair measure; aye; I fancy; hush now lad; over yonder.*
* Jacob's accent as shown in the spelling of the words: *'tis a hard and dangerous course* and *aye.*
* Riddles: *Now there's a tale ... I was sent for by a little bird ... the sweetest little bird; Close as an oyster that's me.*
* Construction and syntax of the sentences: *...and there's heartbreak in it somewhere, I'm thinkin'; happen I may be around.*

At the end of this work, discuss how using this type of language helps the reader to visualize the character, and then end the discussion with a comparison between language then and now.

GROUP WORK

Both Ann and Jacob are very much against Dickon being involved with the bear cub. They feel it is dangerous and that the Bear Master only wants Dickon involved for money. In differentiated groups, ask the children to think about the arguments for and against Dickon being involved.

The more able children should need little support for this writing, however children who need more support can use the writing frame on photocopiable page 28, 'Should Dickon be involved with the bear cub?' In both cases, encourage the children to come to their own conclusions 'for' or 'against' Dickon being involved, by balancing their arguments.

PLENARY

Ask different children to share their opinions about Dickon's involvement and to give reasons why they have come to their personal conclusion.

LESSON PLANS

ELIZABETHAN LONDON – THE TIME AND PLACE
PLOT SUMMARY: CHAPTER SIX

Dickon has promised Ned, his friend from the tannery, that he will go to Southwark Fair with him on Saturday. Dickon now regrets making this promise but goes along anyway. As they enter the streets, full of food stalls, Ned announces he wants to go to the Bear Garden and see the baiting. He also knows a way in without having to pay. Dickon hates it inside and finds it violent and repulsive, so he goes to find the bear cub, leaving Ned behind. Ned follows him, sees him with the cub and accuses him of sorcery. Ned leaves saying he will tell Master Nashe, and as he leaves Osric enters.

RESOURCES NEEDED

Pages 80 and 81 of *A Boy and His Bear* prepared as OHTs (optional), photocopiable page 29, a collection of information books on Elizabethan life, pupils' individual glossary sheets (photocopiable page 23).

WHOLE-CLASS WORK

This chapter sets the scene of Elizabethan London. It takes the reader through a London fair and then on into the Bear Garden. The description of the bear baiting is quite graphic and needs to be discussed with the class. Establish that the description is so violent, that Dickon's adverse reaction is clearly justified, and that his subsequent determination to stop his bear cub from enduring that fate at all costs is well founded. Discuss also the relationship between Dickon and Ned – and how Ned's role in all of this has strained their friendship. Ask the class to predict what will happen in the next chapter as Harriet Graham has left the storyline on a cliffhanger.

Return to the description of the stalls on pages 80 and 81. If possible, use OHTs of the two pages to focus discussion on what sort of words are used to describe the goods the stalls are selling: *gingerbread, red apples, pears, onions, cloth, ribbons, lavender* and *ducks and pigs*.

Look at the paragraph on page 81 beginning 'Dickon didn't want to run ...' This paragraph is made up of a series of complex sentences. Draw the children's attention to the long third sentence, punctuated with commas and semi-colons. Ask them to identify the stalls and their wares that are listed. Go back to the beginning of the

LESSON PLANS

paragraph and identify each of the six sentences – where they start and stop. The first two and the last two frame the description of the stalls. With the children, identify how the clauses and phrases are connected.

GROUP WORK

In differentiated groups, ask the children to think about how the author sets the time and place within the story. Link this to the work on Jacob, and the way he speaks. Ask the children to categorize the information under the different headings on photocopiable page 29, 'How do we know the story is set in Elizabethan England?', in relation to style of talking, people's names, food, transport, pastimes and work. Ask the more able children to consult appropriate reference books to compare the information given. Is it the same? Are there any differences? If so, why might that be?

PLENARY

Share and brainstorm with the class the information they have found out from the book. Encourage them to think about how the time differs from the present day. Finally, discuss with the children their developing glossaries (let them continue on the back of the sheet) and compare definitions of the same word.

SUPERSTITION

PLOT SUMMARY: CHAPTERS SEVEN AND EIGHT

Osric approaches the door of the barn in a sinister manner. He acts in a very threatening way and throws Dickon into the same cage as the cub and she-bear, who has just returned terribly injured from fighting in the ring. Dickon is knocked unconscious and is about to be attacked by the she-bear, but is saved by the cub from being killed. The Bear Warden, Fulke, manages to get Dickon out of the cage. Meanwhile, Ned has fetched Master Nashe, who comes to the Garden to ask about Dickon. Everyone denies knowledge of seeing him. Fulke is worried about Dickon's safety and so he decides to go and fetch Jacob to help. Meanwhile, Dickon is left hiding in the hay loft, but Osric finds him and accuses him of witchcraft. Osric then sets the stable on fire. Dickon is saved with the cub and is helped to escape from the gathering mob by Jacob.

BACKGROUND INFORMATION

Elizabethans were very superstitious of unusual acts or unusual people. They believed that when people performed any acts against others, which could not be easily or logically explained, then their work was really sorcery. Some thought that witches went against God, sold their souls to the devil or had made a pact with the devil. However, historians today believe that an Elizabethan was more likely to be hanged for stealing than for being found a witch!

RESOURCES NEEDED

Flip chart, paper, writing materials.

WHOLE-CLASS WORK

Begin with a general discussion about the events which lead to Dickon running away with the cub. Ensure that the children understand that it was not just Dickon's desire to help the cub that made him run away. Other factors towards his dislike of the tannery were the fact that he would soon have to use the knife and his being accused of sorcery. Re-read the description of the visit to church on page 55, and then discuss the influence of religion in Elizabethan times.

LESSON PLANS

Tell the children a little about Elizabethan superstitions in order to help put Osric's accusation that Dickon had strange powers into context. Within this section of the story, several people believe Dickon has special powers because he can do something unusual:

> Ned: "'Tis the devil's work you do here" and "'Tis unnatural."
> Master Nashe: "... For this apprentice, OUR apprentice, mark you, has bewitched your bear cub."
> Mistress Nashe: "'Tis the devil's work, I'd say."
> Osric: "Quiet, devil's brat," Osric cut in, his voice soft and low. "No more of your tricks. First you bewitched the she-bear's whelp. Now you have bewitched the Master."

List the vocabulary linked to witches and go on to discuss the root word 'witch' and the family of words that develop from it, with the addition of prefixes and suffixes, such as witches, witchery, witchcraft, bewitch, bewitched, bewitches. Point out to the class how adding a prefix such as 'be-' can change the word from a noun to a verb.

Finally, discuss with the children how they think Dickon is really controlling and teaching the bear cub.

GROUP WORK

In differentiated groups, ask the children to write character descriptions of one of the following characters: Fulke the Bear Warden, the Bear Master, Osric, Master Nashe, Mistress Nashe. For less able children, you might identify for them where their character features in the book. Encourage the children to refer to the text to support their opinions. Children who complete the description quickly might go on to compare two different characters.

PLENARY

Discuss what we know about the characters and the differences between them. Then ask the children to predict what will happen next in the story.

SHAKESPEARE'S WORLD
PLOT SUMMARY: CHAPTER NINE

Dickon and Jacob escape through the dark streets with the bear cub in a hamper. As they make their way to a wagon that Jacob has organized, two figures come out of a tavern. Jacob says they are actors from the Globe theatre. One, called Will, stops to talk to Jacob. From here, Dickon and the cub are put in a wagon, going to Deptford with a troupe of French acrobats. The next morning when Dickon wakes, the wagon has stopped next to the Thames. The bear cub is allowed into the river and it is decided that Dickon and the cub can go with the acrobats to France.

BACKGROUND INFORMATION

It is implicit that the character Will in this chapter is William Shakespeare. The Globe Theatre, which is discussed here, was built in 1597 but burned down in 1616. It is said that Shakespeare included the bear in his play *The Winter's Tale* because there was a famous bear performing at the Bear Garden and he wanted to give it a walk-on part.

LESSON PLANS

RESOURCES NEEDED
Poster, photocopiable page 30, writing materials.

WHOLE-CLASS WORK
Talk to the class about William Shakespeare, the Globe theatre and the play *The Winter's Tale*. Read the extract from the Leon Garfield story version of *A Winter's Tale* given on the poster. Then go on to look carefully at the short extract from the actual play on the poster. Identify words and phrases that are interesting and unusual, such as '*but my heart bleeds*', '*The day frowns more and more*' and '*A savage clamour*', and then discuss their meaning.

Now look at pages 142–143 of *A Boy and His Bear*. Ask the children what we learn about Shakespeare's character from the extract. Does Shakespeare know that there is a cub in the hamper? What does he think of apprentices?

GROUP WORK
In differentiated groups, ask the children to do the work on the extract from page 147 given on photocopiable page 30, 'Looking closely at description'. Less able children may read the extract through, identify the adjectives and then rewrite it in their own words. Encourage the children to read the extract and discuss it as a group. Then move on to the others activities on the photocopiable sheet: looking at adjectives, the use of metaphor and finally work on inference and deduction. Some children may find the work on metaphors too demanding and thus further work on similes may be more appropriate.

PLENARY
Discuss with the children the difference between metaphor and simile. Share some examples. End by discussing the significance of the closed hamper.

THE ESCAPE TO FRANCE
PLOT SUMMARY: CHAPTERS TEN AND ELEVEN
The acrobats take Dickon and the cub with them to France. They dock at Mimizon in South-West France and make their way to Orthez. Here they perform and Dickon plays his flute. Dickon catches a brief glimpse of the Bear Catcher, but he tells no one. As it is autumn, the grapes are being picked but there is no work for the troupe, so they make their way to the safety of the mountains. Rosa has named the cub Nounou. Dickon is happy, but is suspicious of Bruno. Rosa says it is just his manner. Autumn slips into winter and the cub sleeps for two months. When he wakes, he has changed and is almost fully grown. Dickon and Rosa constantly try to encourage him to dance but fail. One day when Sebastien is away, Dickon is attacked by someone with a knife.

RESOURCES NEEDED
A map showing Great Britain and France, with Mimizan marked (Mimizon in the book). Mimizan is between Bordeaux and Bayonne in South-West France. A cut-out of a sailing boat, Blu-Tack, photocopiable page 31, writing materials, an OHT of the bear's narrative on pages 175–176 (optional).

WHOLE-CLASS WORK
Use the map to show the class where the troupe have gone to in France, moving the sailing boat along the route. Secure it in place on the map using Blu-Tack. Explain that the name which Rosa gives the bear – Nounou – is similar to the French word for 'teddy bear'. Go on to look at the bear's narrative and what he is

LESSON PLANS

feeling about Dickon. Discuss with the children if they think his feelings have changed: 'He has brought me out of the place of darkness and blood. So I do his will.' (page 158). Examine the extract at the beginning of Chapter Eleven and discuss what the bear cub is feeling and thinking. This might be put onto an OHT, to allow for a more detailed analysis. From this, identify the vocabulary associated with bears – *snout, claws, fur, hibernation* – and also the information that has been learned about what they eat and how and where they used to live.

GROUP WORK

In this part of the story, Dickon has built up a relationship with three new people – Rosa, Sebastien and Bruno. Ask different groups to choose one of these characters and to write about Dickon from his or her perspective. Let the children pool their ideas, but write independently. Ask the groups to write three diary entries for their chosen character – when the character first meets Dickon in London; when the group are in Orthez; when they are living in the mountains. Ask the children to consider what Dickon looks like, the sort of person he is, his relationship with the bear and whether the character wants him with the troupe. After twenty minutes, ask the children to read through their pieces for sense and errors. Photocopiable page 31, 'What do Sebastien, Rose and Bruno think of Dickon?', will give support to those children who need it. Differentiation is by outcome but less able children may only be able to write one or two diary entries. More able children should be directed to write from Bruno's perspective.

PLENARY

Organize the children into groups of three, each child having written about a different character. Ask each trio to compare their diary entries. Then, as a class discuss the similarities and differences in the three characters' perception of Dickon, according to the children's findings.

LESSON PLANS

CAPTURE AND FREEDOM
PLOT SUMMARY: CHAPTERS TWELVE AND THIRTEEN

The Bear Catcher kidnaps Dickon, Rosa and Nounou. He has been following them since they visited Orthez. He takes the three of them far into the mountains, to a secret location. Throughout these chapters, the Bear Catcher is portrayed as a despicable man and Dickon blames himself for the situation. When they reach the destination, the Catcher reveals that he wants to use the cub as bait with which to capture other wild bears. Rosa hopes that Sebastien may come to find them, and leaves a trail of stones and then some stones in the shape of an arrow as a message. The Catcher sees the arrow shape, is enraged and raises his whip to lash Rosa. Nounou becomes angry, breaks his rope and runs towards the Catcher, who then falls into the river and drowns. Nounou is thus free. Dickon and Rosa make no attempt to catch him, but watch as he makes his way into the mountains.

RESOURCES NEEDED
Flip chart, dictionaries and thesauruses.

WHOLE-CLASS WORK

At the beginning of this session, ask the children how they felt when the Bear Catcher found Dickon and the cub again. List their feelings and then discuss the different things that the Bear Catcher does to make the reader dislike him, such as holding a knife to Rosa's throat, gagging them and not feeding the bear.

Then focus on pages 221–224 to see how the author builds up our impression of the Bear Catcher, as well as showing that Nounou really is a wild bear. Initially, ask the class to discuss how the Bear Catcher is shown through:

* the use of dialogue: '"Hold your tongue, wench," he snapped.' (page 223);
* his actions: '...the Bear Catcher who still stood, tapping the whip against his leg.' (page 224);
* description of him: 'The Bear Catcher's good humour had gone...' (page 221).

Ask the children to think why the description of the bear reacting in this way has been written in by the author.

GROUP WORK

Nounou has his freedom. Rosa realized that the cub needed freedom – and on page 233 she relates it to their own freedom. In their groups, ask the children to re-read page 234 and to think about what Dickon was thinking and feeling. For a few minutes ask the children individually to brainstorm the sort of feelings he might have, happy to see that Nounou has his freedom, but sad because he is losing him. Let them have access to the dictionaries and thesaurus if they wish.

Then ask the children to write a haiku poem, to show the feelings they have listed. If the children have not written haiku poetry for a while, you might remind them of the form before the hour. Remind the children about using figurative language such as similes and metaphors. As haiku poems are short, the children can be encouraged to redraft their work.

In the last few minutes of group work, ask the children to read through, change and or correct their work, and last of all to think of an appropriate title. Differentiation is by outcome.

PLENARY

Help children think about the process of writing. Share some of Dickon's feelings that the children identified in their brainstorming session. Then share some of the first drafts and finish by reading out the poems, along with their titles. Discuss how this process helps writers mould and craft their work.

LESSON PLANS

THE END AND THE FUTURE
PLOT SUMMARY: CHAPTER FOURTEEN

Rosa and Dickon, left alone, watch Nounou disappear into the mountains. They discuss his freedom and sit for a while waiting to see if he will return to them. But he does not. As they wait Sebastien and Bruno arrive, having followed the trail left by Rosa. They tell Dickon and Rosa how Marie was tricked into telling the Bear Catcher when Dickon would be alone. The four discuss the future and it is decided that Dickon will stay with the tumbling act and play his flute for them. The story concludes with the thoughts of the bear, now free in the mountains where he was born and about to start his real life.

RESOURCES NEEDED

Flip chart, photocopiable page 32, writing materials, examples of reviews of children's books from newspapers and magazines.

WHOLE-CLASS WORK

After reading the chapter, elicit the children's response to the ending. Was it realistic? Did they like it? What do they think will happen to Dickon in the future? If they were the author, what would they write in a sequel?

Then, look back over the story and encourage the class to think about the links that Harriet Graham has put in throughout to tie the narrative together, such as Dickon's ability to play the flute, hating the tannery, being sent to the Bear Garden with the letter, Jacob being on hand to help Dickon and so on. These links help structure the narrative for the reader. They make the plot more interesting and complex, as well as leaving gaps to which the reader can respond.

Finally, ask the children to work in pairs and to focus on particular aspects of the story that they either liked or disliked. They should then report back to the whole class. If possible, try and find the actual sections in the text to share.

GROUP WORK

In differentiated groups, ask the children to summarize the story for a particular audience and purpose.

For the less able groups, ask the children to rewrite the blurb on the back cover, initially re-reading the actual cover blurb and then using the writing frame on photocopiable page 32, 'Writing a blurb for the book cover', as support. The audience should be children like themselves and the purpose is to summarize the story and to attract the reader.

For more able groups, ask them to review the book for the children's section in a national newspaper. The review should include a short synopsis of the plot and two or three sentences of critical review. The review should be no more than 200 words in length. You might like to show children a selection of reviews to illustrate the writing style and content.

PLENARY

Focus the discussion on the process of writing a limited number of words about a long text, what the difficulties were and how the children overcame these. Share some of the synopses from the blurbs and the reviews. Compare a critical response, for example from the reviews to selling points, such as the blurb. What are the similarities and differences?

LESSON PLANS

AFTER READING

'MY MOTHER SAW A DANCING BEAR' BY CHARLES CAUSLEY

RESOURCES NEEDED
Poster, flip chart.

BACKGROUND INFORMATION
Looking at the Charles Causley poem is a fitting conclusion to the work on *A Boy and His Bear*. The content of the poem clearly illustrates what bears were made to do and also where they always wanted to be. The last verse is particularly relevant to the children's work, as the children in the poem see the truth in the bear's eyes.

WHOLE-CLASS WORK
Display the poster and read through the poem. After the first reading, ask the children what their immediate response is to the poem. What did the children feel the poem was about? What were their feelings about a bear dancing for children? How does the dialogue compare to that in *The Boy and His Bear*? Read the poem again and ensure the children's understanding of it by discussing the following questions:

* What did the keeper do?
* What did the keeper make the bear do?
* What were the children's first reactions?
* Why did these reactions change?

At this stage, ask the children to identify any words or phrases that they do not understand, such as *bruin, burning coat of fire, shaming the laughter to stop*. Discuss the meanings and usage.

Explore the rhythm and rhyme in the poem. Read through the poem again with the children joining in. Ask the class to identify the rhyme (ABCB) and write this on a flip chart. Then discuss how some lines do not end with punctuation but run on to the next line. Read these aloud to the children and show how this technique aids reading the poem aloud.

Finally, ask the children to work in threes to perform the poem. This could be achieved by each child taking an alternate verse, or by one child reading the poem and the others performing as either the bear or its keeper.

GROUP WORK
In differentiated groups, ask the children to think about the difference between the bear in the poem 'My Mother Saw a Dancing Bear' and Nounou in the story *A Boy and His Bear*, and then write one or two more verses for the poem. Less able pupils may need to work in the guided group and write only one verse to add to the Causley poem, while more able children could be encouraged to write more and to keep closely to Causley's poetic style. The children could focus on wild bears, like Nounou, living in the distant mountains. The verses should follow the pattern of the Causley poem, four lines, with an ABCB rhyme. A few minutes from the end, ask the children to read the verses through aloud, thus checking them for sense and rhythm.

PLENARY
In this sharing session the children could read out their verses as well as sharing phrases and words with which they were pleased, and saying why. End the session with the groups performing the Causley poem to the rest of the class.

PHOTOCOPIABLE

Name _____   Date _____

PROLOGUE: IN THE BEGINNING...

In your group, read through the 'Prologue' and discuss what you think this word means. Use a dictionary to check.

✸ Now give brief answers to these questions:

Who is talking to us?
_____

Who does the narrator live with?
_____

What do you learn about their lives?
_____
_____
_____

Where do they live?
_____

Who are they afraid of?
_____

What happens at the end of the 'Prologue'?
_____
_____
_____

Can you predict what will happen next?
_____
_____
_____

Summary
✸ Read through your answers and then write a short piece about the 'Prologue' to read out to the rest of the class.

PHOTOCOPIABLE

Name _____   Date _____

EXPLORING DICKON'S CHARACTER

After reading Chapter One with your teacher, you will realize that Dickon is a central character in this story. The story starts in a tannery and then goes back in time.

✸ Describe Dickon's life before his father died. (pages 3–10)
_____
_____
_____

✸ Why do you think Dickon's mother let him go and work in the tannery?
_____
_____
_____

✸ Mistress Nashe thinks Dickon is lazy. Read page 11 in your group and write down all the different words and phrases that are linked with laziness.
_____
_____
_____
_____

Dickon's lazy actions	Dickon's thoughts about laziness
'pulled the blanket over his head'	

✸ Turn to the beginning of the chapter and read to the top of page 3. Fill in this chart. Think about what Dickon does and how he feels about being called lazy. Use the actual words from the book.

✸ Discuss in your group whether you think Dickon is lazy. If you think he is, does he have a right to be lazy?

LITERACY HOUR UNITS — 21 — A BOY AND HIS BEAR

Name _____   Date _____

EXPLORING DICKON'S CHARACTER: EXTENSION

When Dickon is late getting to the yard, Mistress Nashe pushes him under the water pump:

> 'Dickon winced and gritted his teeth as the <u>freezing</u> water <u>gushed</u> over his head. He had learnt that there was no point in <u>wriggling</u> or protesting. The <u>trick</u> was to stay still and try to get his head as far under the <u>spout</u> of water as possible; that way it didn't run down inside his collar. The <u>dousing</u> seemed to last longer than ever that day …' (page 11)

❋ What words tell you that Dickon did not enjoy this experience?
_____
_____
_____

❋ Was this the first time this has happened to Dickon? If not, how do you know?
_____
_____
_____
_____

❋ Read through the short passage again and replace the underlined words with others, but do not change the meaning.
_____
_____
_____
_____

❋ Think about the clues given in the story so far and predict what might happen to Dickon in the future.

❋ Dickon is the name of a character in another well-known children's novel. Find out the title of this novel, who wrote it and when it was written. Tell your teacher what you have found.

A BOY AND HIS BEAR — LITERACY HOUR UNITS

PHOTOCOPIABLE

Name _____   Date _____

GLOSSARY

As you read these words in *A Boy and His Bear,* fill in the meaning in the glossary below. Add other words that you find interesting which are not included in this list.

Word	Page	Meaning
apprenticed	3	
bear's whelp	100	
carcasses	6	
curfew	10	
gabled house	3	
litany	11	
merchant	3	
milksop	7	
salve	117	
sorcery	95	
surcoat	29	
tannery	6	
whetstone	25	
wicket gate	34	

LITERACY HOUR UNITS   A BOY AND HIS BEAR

MEMORIES AND THE PAST (1)

'... Dickon ducked down the steps that led to St Mary's church, away from the press of people. By cutting through the churchyard he would come to Bankside itself.

He knew the churchyard well, for it was here, on Sunday afternoons, that Ann would come and meet him, taking the ferry across the river from Eastcheap. Then they would walk together along the river bank, or sit on the grass sharing the little Sunday cakes that she had made, still warm from baking and wrapped in a napkin. Sometimes she brought a bunch of flowers to put on their father's grave, for he had been born in Southwark and it was here that he was buried. The grass had quite grown over the place now, of course, but the lettering on the stone was still newly chiselled and bold. "Richard Stronge. Merchant of London. Died 6th July in the year of Our Lord 1597."'

(page 23)

MEMORIES AND THE PAST (2)

'"I saw Jacob last week," she said. "He has found new work, at the Globe theatre on Bankside."

Taken by surprise, Dickon had stared at her.

"You mean our Jacob? Our Jacob is an actor?"

"Not exactly." Ann smiled. "He helps in the tiring house, where the actors change into their costumes for the play. And he moves the scenery. You know Jacob ... he can turn his hand to many things."

"Oh I should so like to see him," Dickon said.

"He sent you his greetings," Ann said, "and wondered how you did at your studies."

"And when you told him that I am now apprentice to Master Nashe – what did he say?"

"Not much," Ann said. "Just wrinkled up his face like a sour apple and harrumphed." She did an imitation of him and they both laughed.

Jacob had been part of their family, and Dickon had missed him almost as much as he had missed his father. Many a time, when he was younger, Jacob had carried him on his shoulders to see the great ships at anchor in the Pool of London, and when his sledge ran against a stone step and splintered, it had been Jacob who mended it for him.'

(page 25)

PHOTOCOPIABLE

Name _____   Date _____

DICKON'S THOUGHTS ABOUT THE BEAR CUB

At the end of Chapter Three, Dickon finds himself in a difficult situation. If he does not work with the cub, it will be killed, but he does not have any free time.
✹ Read his thoughts and then answer the questions below.

'Too young to be killed like that, Dickon thought, turning to look once more at the cub … his cub, a pathetic bundle of brown fur that sat, watching him, its head to one side. He must do something … but what? His mind raced.
"A pity," the Master said. "But there we are. You are apprenticed to Master Nashe, as you say. And your master, the Tanner, has sent a letter asking when I shall have a bear hide for him, no doubt."
He had pulled the letter out of his pocket by then and was reading it through. Already, Dickon thought, it was too late. He looked at the cub again and swallowed. His throat felt tight and dry, and his heart was pounding. There must be a way to save the cub. But how?
Then, quite suddenly, the idea slipped into his mind.'
(pages 48–49)

✹ Now answer these questions.

What did Dickon think? _____
_____

Why was his throat dry and his heart pounding? _____
_____

Why did he keep looking at the cub? _____
_____

How was the cub described? _____
_____

What made the Master get out the letter when he did? _____
_____

PHOTOCOPIABLE

Name _____   Date _____

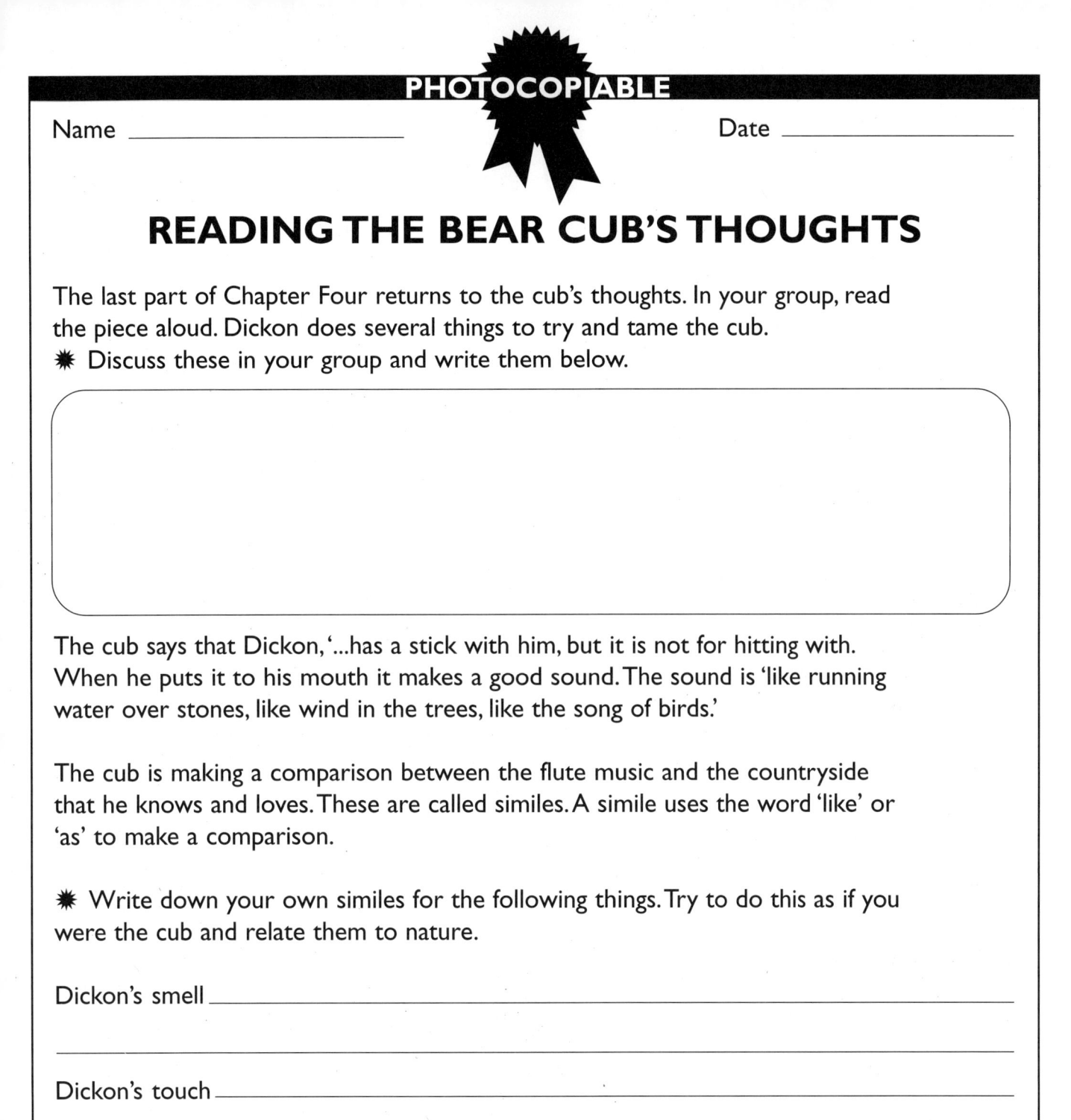

READING THE BEAR CUB'S THOUGHTS

The last part of Chapter Four returns to the cub's thoughts. In your group, read the piece aloud. Dickon does several things to try and tame the cub.
✸ Discuss these in your group and write them below.

The cub says that Dickon, '...has a stick with him, but it is not for hitting with. When he puts it to his mouth it makes a good sound. The sound is 'like running water over stones, like wind in the trees, like the song of birds.'

The cub is making a comparison between the flute music and the countryside that he knows and loves. These are called similes. A simile uses the word 'like' or 'as' to make a comparison.

✸ Write down your own similes for the following things. Try to do this as if you were the cub and relate them to nature.

Dickon's smell _____

Dickon's touch _____

The feeling when the straps are taken off _____

The taste of the food _____

The feeling when Dickon leaves _____

LITERACY HOUR UNITS   A BOY AND HIS BEAR

PHOTOCOPIABLE

Name _____   Date _____

SHOULD DICKON BE INVOLVED WITH THE BEAR CUB?

Both Ann and Jacob feel that Dickon should not become involved with the bear cub.

✸ Complete the frame below.
Write the opinions of Ann and Jacob in the 'against' column and Dickon's opinion in the 'for' column.
Once you have done this, think about the different opinions and write you own opinion in the last box.

Against being involved	For being involved
Ann's opinion is:	Dickon's opinion is:
Jacob's opinion is:	

My opinion is:

A BOY AND HIS BEAR — LITERACY HOUR UNITS

PHOTOCOPIABLE

Name _____   Date _____

HOW DO WE KNOW THE STORY IS SET IN ELIZABETHAN ENGLAND?

By now you should have a feel for the time in which this story is set. How has the author, Harriet Graham, achieved this feel? Skim the six chapters you have read and find examples for the following:

style of talking

people's names

food

transport

pastimes

people's work

When you have completed the chart look again at the glossary you are keeping and record any new words that you have found.

EXTENSION
Now look through an information book about the reign of Queen Elizabeth I. Check to compare the information in it about Elizabethan England with what you have found out from the author of *A Boy and His Bear*.

Name _____   Date _____

LOOKING CLOSELY AT DESCRIPTION

'It was a fine morning, pale and bright. Already the sun was scattering the early morning mist, and down below he could see the river, broader now and silver blue, with the tall masted sailing ships riding at anchor. Beside the wagon, which was drawn up on the grass, the road wound towards Deptford. Sitting a little way off on the trunk of a fallen tree beside the stream were Sebastien, Bruno and Rosa, and next to them was the hamper, still closed.'
(page 147)

✳ Read through this extract and highlight the adjectives that help describe the scene.

In this extract, sailing ships are described as: 'tall masted sailing ships riding at anchor.'
✳ Write this sentence in your own words and try to and use adjectives to describe what you mean.

_____

_____

The writer has also used metaphor within this piece, such as: 'Already the sun was scattering the early morning mist.' A metaphor is similar to a simile but it doesn't use 'like' or 'as': it says one thing **is** another. Here the sun seems to have the ability to scatter the mist. The scattering happens because the sun is almost melting the mist, that is pushing it away.

✳ Think about these objects listed below and try to write metaphors to describe them. The first one is completed for you:

The river	–	a silver ribbon winding through the countryside.
A sailing ship	–	
A wagon	–	
A candle	–	
An actor	–	
A stream	–	

✳ Read the last sentence in the above extract again. What does putting the words 'still closed' after the comma do here? And why do you think the hamper was still closed?
✳ Write your ideas down on the back of this sheet.

A BOY AND HIS BEAR — LITERACY HOUR UNITS

PHOTOCOPIABLE

Name _____   Date _____

WHAT DO SEBASTIEN, ROSA AND BRUNO THINK OF DICKON?

✷ Write three diary entries about Dickon, from the point of view of either Sebastien, Rosa or Bruno.

✷ Circle who you are writing as: **Sebastien   Rosa   Bruno**

As you write about Dickon, describe what you think about: what he looks like, what he is like as a person, his friendship with the bear cub, what the other members of the troupe think of him; whether you want him to join the troupe and play music.

London

Orthez

In the mountains

✷ Once you have written your diary entry, read it through to be sure it makes sense.

LITERACY HOUR UNITS   A BOY AND HIS BEAR

PHOTOCOPIABLE

Name _____   Date _____

WRITING A BLURB FOR THE BOOK COVER

When writing a blurb for the back of a book, you have to write very clearly and not write too much.

✹ Read the back cover blurb of *A Boy and His Bear* to remind yourself of the style of writing.

✹ Now write three or four sentences that will tell the reader about the story. Who is the main character? When and where is it set? What is the story about? Don't forget you want to give the reader some information as well as leaving some questions unanswered.

✹ Now make up two or three 'quotations' from newspaper reviews to add to the cover, to attract the reader's attention and to use as selling points.

✹ When you have finished, read through, correct your work and share it with your partner.

A BOY AND HIS BEAR — LITERACY HOUR UNITS